ascent

poems

doris davenport

*With gratitude
& laughter,
always,
doris*

Copyright © 2011 by doris davenport
All rights reserved.

ISBN: 1463786131
ISBN-13: 9781463786137

Manufactured in the United States of America
FIRST PRINTING

Cover design & section illustrations: Audrey Davenport
Interior photos: doris davenport unless otherwise indicated

This publication was partly made possible by support from the Artistic Assistance Program of Alternate ROOTS (Arts-Community-Activism).   http://alternateroots.org

To purchase additional copies:
        https://www.createspace.com/3652184
        amazon.com & other retailers
        d.davenport: zorahpoet7@gmail.com

Printed by CreateSpace, Charleston SC

also by doris davenport

poetry

it's like this, 1980
eat thunder & drink rain, 1982
Mangia il tuono e bevi la pioggia, 1988
    (Italian translation *of eat thunder* . . .)
voodoo chile, slight return, 1991
Soque Street Poems, 1995
madness like morning glories, 2005
a hunger for moonlight, 2006
sometimes i wonder, 2010

contents

abstergent — 1

(another) security check	5
Tribute to Suzan-Lori Parks' *365 Days / Plays*	6
At ASU one day	7
to do this (write abt you, Sherley Anne Williams)	8
chiropractor list:	9
Torch 18/4/08	10
for SEAN BELL	11
Friends at MELUS* (Columbus, OH 2008)	13
Praise Poem to a Head of Cabbage	14
Memorialize this (26/5/2008)	15
Tiara # 2	16
YAAAY! (4 June 2008)	17
17 syllables (plus one) of good feelings	18
Stilt Walking at ROOTs Annual Meeting (astca)	19
Sometimes i forget	20
Miriam Makeba	21
you caught me	22
The Inauguration of President Obama	23
If then, there is no	25
Dr. W. Rice	26
This morning is hard	27
"Lifting the Veil" - A CNN Special	28
George Washington Carver Park	29
Another Memorial Day	31
something like sleep	32
nerd confession # 7	32
well then	33

hot (another list)	34
Learn to fly a plane	35
then there's this (April 2010)	36
A Bodyguard Speaks	37
"What do you do there?" he asked.	38
Randomly opened a new book of	39

text in body   41

one of the first	44
walking text-poems for Charquita Arnold	44
and if i asked one of them	45
a (2 lap) hunt	46
oops. pardon me: just bumped	47
translucent fidgety fingers	48
Knowing very little actually about	48
raindrops keep bouncing off	50
Long strides relieve	50
the miracle of the oak	50
measuring steps	51
huge turtle shell, big grey rock.	52
Earth Day #1 2011	52
NAL poem	52
This Morning's Ambitions	53
where it was going	54
for yestrdy	55
stuck screaming sluggish	55
thick heavy thighs	55
bluebell blue ribbons bow-tied	55
like this picture	57
poem @ 10 o'clock	58
after the 6 hr drive from	58

17 (more) Grateful Syllables for Hisaye	59
performance (headwrap) piece for Kay B.	60
tall green lake rushes	61
listen - hear them - giggle:	61
dance thought - (another) giggle	61
tired of love	61
It wanted a name too (The Tuscaloosa Tornado)	62
4 July 2011	63
in this glorious morning	64
friday	65
Hidden Stream Park, West Baltimore	65
Dennis was his name i think & i can	67
unnameable	68
Fathers' Day (for D. Patton & Lisa Saurez)	69
Another Sunday @ the lake	69
sacred space small depot	70
Invocation (29/3/2011)	71
for Zelda Lee (& her knee operations)	72
can't get away from	73
Thursday: for Oya, Damballah, Chango	73
85 degrees already	74
today is (for Gil Scott-Heron 28 May 2011)	74
the farmvle blues	75

ascent 77

Erik Satie piano music poem	79
glimmering desire	80
Toni Morrison's observation	81
My sister Dolores' Birthday	82
Song under the Stillman Magnolias	83
that epic southern novel i promised you	84

to Audrey in Savannah	*86*
Bo Didley dead today at age 79	87
people watch # 7	88
a Pilates Method approach	89
Do not intend to get "old"	89
6 June 2008	90
A Summer Solstice	91
for Li Ch'ing - Chao	92
task:	92
Beach Blues	92
Honorific parody of Maya Angelou's "Still I Rise"	93
Incident at a Red light	95
2 November 2008	96
Conversation with a ladybug	97
TRUST	98
assent	99
self-affirmation ?	101
poem @ 60 / 60 yr old poem	101
the mere thought of	102
and i got a ph.d for this	103
Rubber rain boots with roses	105
"I got things to do . . .	106
my new tattoo at 4 weeks & 1 day old	107
Aw hell, EB	108
maps	*109*
for us	110
Sixty grey and brown	110
ascent	111
Dedication	*112*
About the Author	114

abstergent

abstergent:

a. wiping; cleansing n. anything which cleanses,
    as lotions or soap

- Webster's New Universal Unabridged Dictionary, 1983

(subtitle: let the alligator win)

(another) security check

the diminutive pale Euro-looking Hispanic grins
oh there's Hedwig (my backpack) phonily gushes
your hair is so pretty (yes i know)
pats me down, violated i travel
elsewhere in my head turned

sharp left a small female Asian, seven or eight years old,
so thin almost invisible sideways being wand-frisked
up and down little stick arms straight to her sides tiny
legs spread apart on the mat-with-foot placement quick
switch to the right: a

fully purdah'ed brown Muslim womon
in darker brown clothes covering arms, legs,
face Muslim wimpled patted head-down by a
grinning middle aged whitewoman the little Japanese girl,

the brown Muslim lady and me the only three wimmin
singled out for search doubly suspect by skin, cultural markers,

her & her mother's eyes, the clothes; my bracelets and hair
suspicious because not inconspicuous like *invisible* ethnics
who uneasily grin, smirk, talk mindlessly, feel us up,
chain themselves down.

Tribute to Suzan-Lori Parks'
365 Days / Plays

Set the clock for
five, get up at seven
drink salt water & read abt
Obama. your
decision again:
here or there
sweat anywhere
the same Alice
Walker says
vote for truth

collecting income
tax data as parts of me
try to
live and
die at
the same time

mostly, this
is too trite
too silly for
words as
again i (file an extension and)
stop.

At ASU one day

They told me,
my "upper classmen students"
that morning, that Maya Angelou, at 80,
still teaches. Snidely
LaQueashia Jones asks "You think
you'll still be teaching
@ 80, Dr. D?"

Undoubtedly, i answer & think, as long as
some folk are as dumb as you, as long as
i breath, i teach.

My (mostly) beloved students mock me
to my face say poisonous things with a big
grin, "Uh - huh, you crazy." "You flunk people."
"You hard." Quite a few mock my mannerisms
imitate my hair, head twitch, voice inflections,
a penchant for the word "scholar," which i *will*
occasionally, use with inflected sarcasm to
remind them of what they ain't (scholar)
which one used, just now,
with an intonation of b***h:
"How are you my elderly *scholar*?"
and then, "No, you're a *sage*."

They do, i swear,
worry me, my
most(ly) beloved scholars.

to do this
(write abt you, Sherley Anne Williams) i must

revisit battle sites
of 25 years gone re-
live injuries
sustained see
scorched earth where
some of my mind lies
quivering under debris
still talkn to itself
"das some shit.
das some shit! Git up"
gently caress that
ground-covered kudzu
nudge frontal lobe with
steel tipped
combat boot, peer thru
fight-derived dirt & dust
air swirls, step over
carrion of dead
dreams of critical
community and, like any
epic womon warrior, wearing
a tattoo tale on her
back, part 2 on her tongue, & the
future seared to the back of her
eyeballs, sit down,
sip tea, and
write (this).

chiropractor list:

left knee cap
right neck
right scalens
    shoulders
stuck 90 degrees
C 2-7. occipit.
ow. right wrist.
lower back.
pepsi.
fried kale in
olive oil & sea salt.

Torch   18/4/08

I

China's inhumane acts of aggression toward Tibet created
a peripatetic Olympic Torch run - no one wants it seems
the pc (politically correct) thing is douse it. Be righteously
indignantly pro-Tibet. How come people keep passing
America's torch? (No body no country stops trading with the
USA b/c of its crimes against humanity.)

II

That fundamentalist misogynist "Christian" sect in TX -
whitewimmin & girl-children systematically abused,
physically, psychologically, legally just wondering - *do* these
wimmin have any rights? (Their children removed; the lawyers
protest something else) Where is their refused Torch?

III

Learned, recently, that an ancient law for Chinese
poetry was include nothing ugly. Soon i shall be
classic and Chinese. Until then, light, and pass this torch.

IV

Back to you then

for SEAN BELL
(50 bullets / one artist/ we are all Sean Bell)

(Sean Bell was murdered in Queens, NY, in Nov. 2006; he & two friends, leaving Sean's bachelor party, were shot 50 times by five cops. In 2008, three of the cops were acquitted. This poem was written as part of a protest event by artists-activists in Atlanta, Ga in November or December 2009; an event protesting another travesty of justice. Alice Lovelace invited me to participate & i sent a draft of this poem.)

Like giant jagged lightning
bolts split the sky
in a deadly summer storm in Georgia,
50 bullets split Sean's
soul, spirit, body in another (random) outbreak of
"whitemale pathological privilege,"

his executioners' acquittal splits my
brain sliced heart split pelvic bone separated
(PAIN! PAIN! PAIN!)

as you try to mouth
one word: What, you reckon, that last
could be in a brain
shot into slivers?   *Whatdfuk? Why? Whaaaaa ???*
Not just kill
but annihilate
Sean's *essence*

here, in any afterlife-reincarnation
(he can't never come back) 50 bullets of
whitemale perp-killers' insecurities
institutionalized rationalized
accepted & acquitted of
1-2-3-4-5-6-7-8-9 10 little no, wait, big resentments:
"Black man, plural. Look good. Better'n me. Laughing.
Having fun. Cars newer than." Is that 10 yet or 20 & shoot him
one mo time for being uppity & for the one

running for president only whitemale supremacist
partiarchial psychos allowed are we at 30 bullets yet?
Well,

"Who do you think *you* are? Who you/representing?" The post-traumatic stress disorder of being a loaded whitemale with a itch to fire OH   - *WAIT A MINIT* - hunting rules changed. permits now issued - (not for "thug-gangstahs" who receive awards, accolades, invitations to lecture no longer extant or threatened species but the devolved desired designation of the blackmale no not *them* no more) for ones who look - well - decent, normal - them. Shoot them. On sight. Hunt them down are

you having fun? Are you colored and having fun? Are you *near* a blackmale, fe-male, bar, restaurant, outdoors at nite, at dusk, at dawn and look like you might smile or have fun in clothes that fit you well or almost do you even *think* about being near a place to celebrate have something to smile about or have fun well
            oh. snap. SNAP! We are the targets. Oh -
            bang. (a whole lotsa bangs.)   i am
            the target. i am it. then
            you it.
            you   next.

Friends at MELUS* (Columbus, OH 2008)

At the Varsity bar
last night, he
sat between us.

This morning
i brought her
coffee, she gave me
candy in the
afternoon.

In the afternoon,
she brought me
candy.

*(*Society for the Study of Multi-Ethnic Literature)*

Praise Poem to a Head of Cabbage

O you sweet
delight love of my life in
yesterday's early afternoon calling
me soft, wetly sprinkled deep
green wide leaves open wide
soft whispery "pick me. pick me."
luscious darkgreen holding a richness of
roundness promise of layers of delight
inside o yes, oh you,
my cabbage, you sweet
Tuesday afternoon treat.

Memorialize this (26/5/2008)

Create a time of no war no testosterone driven penis-ego memorialization of death diseased stench of napalmed balls in fantasy strung out to dry no rows & rows of deadmales countries counting coup on unnamed millions of children, martyred nameless wimmin
no more war crimes sanctioned unsanctioned hate crimes: Jews, Queers, African Americans, Wimmin, Poor People, the Elderly, the Young . . . .

Create and remember a "time" of no war.
Memorialize (centuries) of peace.

Tiara # 2

This strong lake front breeze
full of duck feathers and us
nevertheless, peace.

YAAAY! (4 June 2008)

This should be a song, a sound of joy and celebration but no sound is big enough no drink stiff enuf no outlet *out* enough for this: Obama won that one. This far, he won. Even if the racist rag of a newspaper here buried the news on page six, even if that 4w contender gets as much ink as he; although all the isms still gridlock the world, and the minds and souls of my world lit students, still, i say, today, i will rejoice and write, doggerel, about it. So there. Yaaay.

17 syllables (plus one) of good feelings

feeling good feeling
good feeling feeling feeling
good. one more time
again.

Stilt Walking at ROOTs Annual Meeting (astca)

Let me cross that
Bainbridge island bridge
sleep in a space
populated with spiders
i trust the

ground only to rise up
& strike me.

Sometimes i forget

that i am a non-smoking
sober alcoholic & as i
write with my right hand
reach with the left for a
shot glass of tequila
or tall glass of white Italian
wine, my perpetually lit cigarette
and you, my sweet-
kneed Norma.

Miriam Makeba

1932-2008

you caught me

rubbing the spine
of my book-to-be
caressing my
imagination, nurturing
what is to be
b/c oh yes
we did.

oh yes - therefore -
i can.

The Inauguration of President Obama & my 60th (almost) Birthday 18 Jan. 2009 & one of many grocery store water-jug filling poems . . .

Convinced i cld feel the seismic movements of this celebratory change sweeping the world i did nothing except prepare to be someplace with people smiling, grinning, slapping fives yes we did / again & again eyes locked in success, victorious commitment Hugh Masekela's "Promise of a Future" Nina's "New World Coming" / Biblical post-apocalyptic jump up joy because the beast is dead or at least metaphorically deposed, gone (yet in this dismal small town / where joy seems outcast, smiles suspect/ Afrikans not *yet* allowed to celebrate Lincoln's Freedom so how they gone be free for Obama's?)

(*Deeep breath.*)

This *miracle* for the world / not just on the Hudson River conned, soothed, lulled into tip-of-my-nose myopia, forgot all about my Washington DC connections ohhhh Katana what kind of dance will you do now oh my poet-buddy what will you write and Madman - yr analysis? Consider this beyond-words joy this time to celebrate unprecedented, undocumented and now

in this grocerystore where all the Africans do that surreptitious sideways stare pretending they blind to my Obama hat - where? *Where* to be for my 60th anniversary of birth, of we came this far *what* we gone do next of being in love with someone whose world i intend to rock, crack, & re-create, of *living* as a poet, according to the Goddess of my understanding, being a

"60 yr old hottie" according to another person's understanding then what, where, *who* to do to lock in these blessings & keep on being my own miracle, *too* wonderful sweet non-stop (say it say it say it / someday we'll be togeeeethur) rain. blessings like raindrops rich as moonbeams, steady as Mt. Yonah up there in Sautee, rolling thru with the Obama Express, my *own* Hogwarts Express this train i'm on / just picking up speed / heading here with a huge laugh at me / locked down by the mundane still / intending to be free / still thinking i am free.

If then, there is no

If, then, there is no
light or relatively none
in a mind whose darkness compels more
whose despair fills,
breeds, sustains.

If, rising, the body
can withstand the cast
of mind calling back,
come back, and
move through and
well - if i am
here, and no longer
quite there, this
day already blooms
        "success."

prompt: Poets.org's Poem-A-Day, "Yellow Bowl" by Rachel C. Flynn, first line: "If light pours like water / . . ."

Dr. W. Rice

So calmly,
stoically he said
he can walk now -
could not last week.
After his operation he
was paralyzed, he
said, and what
started as prostate
cancer missed
in the colonoscopy has
now pervaded all but
"I am eighty years old.
I've had a good life," he said.
And smiled.

This morning is hard

Winds of basketballs thump
Entropy walks back & forth, back & forth
Newly laid gravel, pebbles
Turpitude, triflingness this Monday morning
Y*awn.*

"Lifting the Veil" - A CNN Special on the "Lives" of Afghan Women

Some women burned themselves
as the single solution to the
sordid wretchedness of their lives

Kerosene, any burning solvent
doused, then lit themselves only to
survive immolation & live scarred, maimed,
disfigured, running pus-scarified faces, shrunken
leg muscles on a 14 year old, sold by her drug addict
father as a bad debt payment when she was 7
now sits sadly on stunted legs under
beady-eyed surveillance
of her sadist jailer-husband

And the poet murdered because her husband
was *jealous* of her fame & popularity & the poet's
brother, in his liquidvoiced English, said the family
"forgave' the man, 5 months jail was sufficient
punishment for his sister-poet's life

Her voice silenced, life taken
theirs crippled, maimed, deformed
enslaved in *this* 21st century
carnival of malepsychosis
horror so total, so global must totally
- like these (inadequate) words -
stop.

George Washington Carver Park & the Sierra Club's Project

> Convinced that urban kids (read "inner city" - code phrase
> for "black & therefore underprivileged" ghetto - whatever term works
> for the liberalmind, the acquiescent colored copy of, right then)

so convinced, the SC sponsors
a series of outdoor treks -
one great big fuzzy
feelgood for all. But

what about us / who already populate(d)
rural areas, country
kids all, barefoot up & down
our hollers landlocked
in the whiteghettoized sickmental
(southern segregationist) need
to sanction off / even air, trees,
dirt: a "Cullud Park." Even now, invisible signs
of "White Only" in the southwest Georgia woods
from the unfenced smallness of our colored (cullud)
park in Northeast Georgia near Toccoa named
for the great & world famous
George Washington Carver who ironically loved &
freely trekked *all* the woods down here, to the deep deep
south of Albany

us country
folk knew and know
the psychic fences, the paranoid
anxiety of going

for an off-the-path
stroll where still we might be
sicced on by dogs, shot
at, chased, raped, eaten,
hung, sh*t, Sierra Club - go head. Let
freedom ring, why doncha. Let
something ring, ring, ring.
(Subtitle: "Naw, i ain't mad.)

Another Memorial Day

> *"At 3 pm Americans asked to take a minute to reflect" . . . to "honor those who died for our freedom"*

Perhaps. Perhaps, also, to
honor those who died, metaphorically, or
literally - who put on the outfit & assumed the
position(s) from lack of purpose, desperation or
dedication to a concept of country.

All the WAC's (Women's Army Corps) & Rosie Riveters back
though history, down through time & up to this minute who
gave male progeny to continue the dubious cause of war while
denigrated & warred upon themselves.

Pause a minute.

Reflect on the females in the un-Democratic National something
somewhere in Africa wimmin repeatedly raped, sadistically
mutilated psychologically, spiritually killed in the path of
somemale's war wait:
play taps for all of them and the sisters in Africa, China, Iran,
Iraq, Amerika, Afghanistan facing acid for a chance to
learn denied access to minds & bodies fully covered oh,
do, "remember the fallen" those who continue
to fall do you remember?
Pause. According to that website the moment of
remembrance was inspired by a child who when asked what is
Memorial Day / said "The day when the swimming
pools open." Let's reflect on that. and this.

something like sleep

sliding into a grey
everythingness floating
beyond a peripherality
becoming (a potato chip
instead of baked potato
casserole maybe)
slipping free of corporeality
always at an angle
still, amazingly, attached
realizing i am out, again,
i slip back in
(to my body)

nerd confession # 7

i like lists.
making them
doing them
crossing them off
starting again like
this for
my ex-crush, Rachel (Maddow):

ergasia
Kavla Shivashankar
laodicean

well then,

        come by here, poem *(tune of Inez & Charlie Foxx's "Come By Here, Boy")*

i could use a little of that
come by here, poem,
everybody wants you but i need
you best - come here.

if i cannot have you
there is no rest today
no purpose
come here, poem.

somebody's hurting, i know,
hurting, praying,
me too: for Jaki's dughter
Imani. for Jaki's daughter Imani come
by here. for Jaki.

Somebody's moaning now,
for real, if that is what it takes.

Come by here, poem.
come by her.

Come here.

hot (another list)

glaring hot
12 noon shootout hot
beatdown hot
beat you down again, hot
in your face hot
make you fight your
grandmomma (& anyone else) hot
sticky hot
"disrespectful" hot
mean hot
ugly hot
sweltering, blistering, endless
pointless hot
vengeful hot
stultifying enervating
humiliating
repressive hot
oppressive hot
day long morning sunrise to 12 midnight gotcha still
sweating hot
don't you dare turn off that
a/c at 3 a.m. hot
& i wld kill myself for some relief (in hell) but
it's too hot to die, hot.

Learn to fly a plane

ride a horse
do my own income tax &
fearlessly ride a
bicycle fast in
car traffic then -
maybe - i won't miss you, Y-the-T,
so much. so badly.

then there's this (april 2010)

(or, i ain't mad # 21)

White dogwood petals stretch
out into empty air like
you in a coffin.

Pink dogwood petals
drift slowly to the ground as
you will too someday.

Spring blossoms once again
and again i see you dead.
Tomorrow's comfort.

A Bodyguard Speaks

I am his bodyguard
and - I just don't like you.
He is kind; I am not.
He is gentle - I hope
you rot in the 9th level of
hell / being made to suck
pus out a corpse's rotten
toenail. I am his
bodyguard and his life is
my job, my sacred
duty and trust. He is
oblique, intelligent, brilliant.
I don't have to be.
I can hurt you. I am
President Barack Obama's
bodyguard. I will *do* you/
badly, permanently.
He - your president -
is kind. I am not.
I am his bodyguard.
His lifeguard, his -
well. I am not
alone. There are millions
of us, globally. (And
on mars and the moon.) And
we *will* get you.

"What do you do there?" he asked.

the mountains of
Western Carolina,
Jekyll Island

i mountain.
i ocean i don't
do. i *be*.

Randomly opened a new book of poetry to see "fried chicken & coffee"

And suddenly
am starving for a
thick plate of fried-
in-heavy-batter chicken, a
hormone engorged breast
& a wing on the side on
the edge of hot, hot
grits, loaded with butter,
pepper, salt. A sausage, 2 home-
made biscuits; 2
eggs over-easy (runny)
& huge mug of scorchin
black coffee to the side
near my left elbow
behind the ashtray where a
lit unfiltered cigarette
burns (Pall Mall or Camels) i
need to shovel this down & maybe seconds on
grits & sausage, then saunter out to the bayou
& rassle me a alligator 'bout a hour
or so / & what da
hay - let that
sucker. win. Yeah.
Let the alligator
win, for once.

text in body

text in body/written walking

around Lake Loretta in Albany, GA mostly

dedicated to my freshman composition students

Introduction:

In February 2011 i got an android touch tone "smart phone" with a full "QWERTY" keyboard. Not that i know what all that means but like Facebook (or rather Farmville) in Nov. 2009, this new techno-toy had a major impact. Especially after i downloaded a writing app.

Inspired by Parks' 365 Days - 365 Plays, i wrote a poem a day (at least) for the last three years. But for most of my life i have kept a small notebook and pen with me, always in writing mode. Now i had/have the "android" (along with pen and paper). i take the phone with me when i walk/ed & the poems wrote thru my body - the rhythm of my stride, transmuted.

Walking and writing "poemetes" is one action. (True performance poetry. Need movement to write, read, understand.) My mind, head, feet, fingers moving as one. Got so smooth, I cld sense a big tree root & avoid it while i saved *and* spoke to people. The poem, the text, was - is - already t/here in my body.

one of the first

experimental works. I
n progress en progress progresn around th lake me, my 5 sisters
virtual sisterhood. see I KNEW ths cld work notall that new
or xperimental i ave alwaays been been walking in a poem
walkn up on. a. poem something
li(k)e that oh wait see ther. is one sister her go another o e
life itscorny but still is experiment at. least. to me what. abt you
this is an xperimental interactivr rc poem. here you go / the timer's.
set. for. you @..com. lol hahaha. u go. no really - yr turn you go . . .

•

*s**s*s***just in cassette I want to practice thief this is no easy
regardless of. how easy some folk make it seminar what is
rjw the secret here? tap n general vicinity?

•

walking text-poems for Charquita Arnold

poems pictures word-photos, 6 a wholefamily of six people
assorted sizes out there already this early pollen pastelgreen
morning as this world decides what to do see what effect
yu hve Miss A (yeah u) to think of u is poetry
well . . . you & MARGAREt Walker 2day
in tree roots & pollen at our lake
of potential possibility promise
let a new day - at least - be writn on the demised debris
of the last. Let's inhale this pollen
choke on its thickness
(this too will pass will b past) &
exhale golden air

and if i asked one of them

what *precisely* is this
rude hard unnatural stare for.
looks of shock disbelief disrespect despair
like i am a ghost or other aberration they lack words &
comprehension for frozen still inside & out eventually
they stutter: "Yo hauh so prittyhowlongittakeutadothat?"
like my new friend Virginia did then "Slang it girl!"
when we passed again & "u so crazee" altho.
it was my hips slanging like a geriatric Tigerette &
Virginia makes "chargers."

a (2 lap) hunt
___

sometimes must go hunting
get out & trak it
down stalk it - today's poem. sweetly cajole & court it ask
how it do and if it *will* do anything
with me today or tease evade run off away
down some other alleyway like
those in ancient Sienna

holler at it like at an old friend spotted on
the other side of Walmart over on fresh meat & u
at the cheese & yogurt coolers but wait here go a dogwood
blooming see how they stand up lift out
offering hey hey can you come &
play in my morning poem for a minit?
or u over in fresh veggies looking for kale & he
on the opposite fresh baked bread & new pastry wall for his
dinner party ears full of expectations deaf to yr
hollah.   Hey Hey!

Like this mist runs across the lake
in front of soft breezes ahead of
accelerating 9 a.m. sun's heat

oops. pardon me: just bumped
into the shadow of an oak tree

•

translucent fidgety fingers
frantic fingers ragged nails rushing feet
hurry hurryhurry. save.

•

Knowing very little actually about

> *(after R. Morgan's poem of the day abt how his father enjoyed working outdoors in the rain . . .)*

the bio-father, mine that is, except he liked
likker, big butted little-minded females
& showing off in multiple ways
on one of his drunk Saturdays or Sundays
(or Tuesdays) but since i too love being out
in the rain drizzle thunder windy chill sprinkle
hard driven giant drops gentle caressing softly falling
mountain misting sideways not right now but in a minute
August dog days drenching downpour to run out barefooted
or bare headed (before I acquired so much hair) or really
just bare head to toe to feel that rain-caress maybe. maybe
some of that predilection dripped down to me,
that and a love of music. maybe.

•

blustery cold wind
blowing down dogwood blossoms
dance up to the sky

●

awful weight of not
alternative worlds collide
sun rise frost
becomes sparkling dew

●

●

Raindrops keep bouncing off
tree leaves, off my Tilley hat brim
drops on my cell phone.
That's not good. That
ain't good atall.

●

Long strides relieve
constricted gluteus maximus
muscles in 2nd stage disc degeneration expect
new pain (daily) but plan to stride on

●

the lesson of the oak :
2 months back brutally
hacksawed down
to ground level
sawed into oblivion
today fifty small shoots
upward

measuring steps

uncountable stars
memorialized lost friends
& found friends
each spot & black hole in my heart counting
longing (lonely) beats of where are you
how could you (cause) this maudlin nostalgic puerile
frozen static carved in smooth purple
alabastr stone written with a stray
stick in summer on hard red dirt
as long as i call yr names you come to me
you will notleave me besides, too brighthot
bug-filled already
out here

huge turtle shell, big grey rock.
an acquaintance from work - her lookalike double
12 noon tortured heat healing cool breeze
the magic of illusions.

Earth Day #1 2011

thick yellow pollen
strangles iron grey lake
yellow tornadoes choke North Carolina
another tsunami starts a nuclear reaction somewhere
a harsh brackish cough
the earth hiccups

NAL poem

(that is, a very esoteric poem requiring copious & learned footnotes for the Norton Anthologies of Lit : Affrilachian, African American, LGBT, American, Women's & World)

we waited a year at a red light
on the way from there to here
one entire year - that stop sign

This Morning's Ambitions

shave my head (again)
weave my wondrous dredlocks
into a magical wig to wear at Full Moons & other holy days.
go sign up for three dance classes-one of them Tap.
howl at the full moon (again) and viv do you think i shld
Come Out - again?

●

where it was going

little black hairy gymnast perp spider
springs out at me opening curtains to this day's light. & it ws
on . . . just like that sprayed toxic smelling poison all over
the area asking forgivness of my flourishing five green plants
held my breath back to desk computer online banking checking
account overdrawn
automatic draft from put-n-take account still too little to cover
ohshit just do it transfer more quik e-mail scan: insulting long
note from bogus publisher must respond (not on today's list.
NOT this day) debilitating. rage wait quik reachout for sistah-
session still did car insurance transfer wait. contact NWU ask
what to do abt recalcitrant publisher. can't must re-subscribe,
pay more $ get new password keep breathing. deep deep get
through send assist e-mail. wait back 2 lizard site automated
humanoid this must be recorded pay mo $pAy more money
unless coerced agree to auto deducts monthly done but can we
just end this session done releasedlaUghter deep breath

in 90 % humidity, 200 % hostility (dam it! just banged my
head twice on low-growing sturdy magnolia lims trying to
avoid swirling balls of bugs, the wht woman pushing a side car
stroller wth 2 babies & a 7 yr old sicklyshirtless boy in front)
well I was bound to run into something but this *is* where I
was going:

bug free insurance card done
boarding pass complete online check in
today I will fly

●

for yestrdy

was abt 2 say this is gettn harder startn
2 feel like work llike another onerous piece of work 2 do.
wth deadlines bbbuilt in as well but then the tornadoes
all across the south & more conce ned abt Stillman than
Soque Street b/c Soque is protected. but spots of T'town
flattened
sumbody. help me I wld say. if there ws eny1 who cld it ain't
let me just get out the wway & tie my shoelaces

●

stuck screaming sluggish
sloppy still. moving on

●

thick heavy thighs
thin fragile feet
agile mind

●

bluebell blue ribbons bow-tied to iron grey mailbx celebrating
somethingsomeone this morning a poem for each hour a color

brightsoft bluedark stonegrey color missing my
Cissy away in Tn wth her bloved horses to play with

so much further that color of missing u is this morning's
streaked wth that sky lonelier now in Sautee since then a
chance to see u maybe coffee here this morning out to lake 2

late walkn around huge tree roots more animated, livelier than these people these who tread methodically wth no headgear no eye protection not noticing the heat not seeing the

great sothwest ga glare yet staring hatefully & full-face& body @ *me* must leave here depart ASAP to somewhere anywhere there may be must b a possibility of a friend wth

whom 2 share a coffee. like Cissy and then a happy grin ran by shouting & waving Gmorning DocDavnport!" & the color shifted: rich deep poetic green algae

like this picture (see?)
(imagine it green. deep rich green)

poem @ 10 o'clock

these actively perturbed faces
march in unjoy around the lake
leadingup to 12 noon
church chimes

the world begins anew
at 2

•

May 1 (or April 30) poem for yesterday

after i read Shalom's poem Ms Leggett sd i shld write abt our
rc intro class . . .

learning 2 trust
learning 2 listen
learning 2 discharge
one session at a time

•

after the 6 hr drive from

Spartanburg in undulating
seductive greenness back to here
thinking if i acknowledge it
it will pass sooner bgone faster exit
thru the air above my heads if i just testify
ackowledge it is baaaaaaad:

O Almighty back pain.
Lower back sacriiliac
and all of the beastie eastie
O reddish raw festering pain like
menstrual cramps for 15 yrs straight
combined pain shoots down left side til
knee buckles pain. o pain.
u de *woemun* AND de man & his momma 2
if that is how you roll.oh. oh.
sharp sharp hot jagged whitepain
migraine til i vomit pain across to my right side
rollercoaster slide swing wigglescream
goodbye goddammit, pain!

•

17 (more) Grateful Syllables for Hisaye

this green morning's buds
remind me of your backyard
tree blooms in California.

the travel postcards
Hong Kong - Japanese bonsai
Bologna towers.

performance (headwrap) piece for Kay B.

wrap a vicissitude around the head (this thing is not. new)

play at the photo shoot

make purple royal
then regal black

red is missing

swag it back
back it up

hear that sound?
contest over?
did i lose?

that is not new.
This ain't new.

tall green lake rushes
one day you have it all ShRon said
and the next it's all gone
in the next tornado minute

•

listen - hear them - giggle:
magnolia trees, sand, gnats.
in on the joke - me.

•

dance thought - (another) giggle

pretending i am
D. Patton on this high kick
with releve . . . ouch.

•

tired of love
stated in a language
i can not comprehend

•

It wanted a name too (The Tuscaloosa Tornado)

they tell me there was one
around 5 a.m. the same day
then that other one 12 hours
later doing a dance of destruction
through five Southern states most
especially Alabama it changed its
mind about moving on they tell
me it came in to town as two funnels
heading straight for our school on the
hill then changed its mind went downtown
this Thing slithered along the ground rose
into the sky gave everyone cognitive dissonance
& despair this Thing needs a
name an entity like this surely if called
by name praised adored
Oh Empress O Divine one. oh . . . god.

4 July 2011

indeed Frederic (Douglass)
still i ponder that absolute query;
"What, to the Slave, is the 4th of July?"
barbecued cholesterol; fake intoxication
false inebriation. amnesia. walking death

●

in this glorious morning

in this glorious morning
never seen or felt before

mark me present universe
rising now in praise

meet me in this ask
growing moon moving parts

goddess song spirit sent
sanctified all day

●

friday

these final imperatives
knocks on the door
soon time to go

●

Hidden Stream Park, West Baltimore

pour libation.
call the spirits.
celebrate this place,
our people. present & gone.
Send in the drums. Dance.

●

Baltimore. oh. baltimore.
Turn left. turn back. Reverse.

●

Dis/Advantages of outside exercise in
200 % humidity, in thick wet air

1. Learn gilled breathing.

2. I ain't no fish.

●

Today's quota met already
O what else shallwe do?
See Holy Sabrika. Git my hair did.

8:20 a.m.

"Here comes the sun
Here comes the sun
Here comes the sun"

and there i go
(it's not allright)

●

Dennis was his name i think & i can

see him just as clear in my mind, Dennis, he walked everwhere
around the hill & downtown him & Miz Anna Tutt
they did you know Dennis- forgot who his people was but
he was short to medium height, medium brown wore overalls
never talked except to say how you or wave
steady walking like he got somewhere to be & don't
mean no harm but ain't got time for you that's how we got
there, walking, maybe sometimes leave way early so you
cld visit wth everyone on the way else they might think
u mad at them unless yr Dennis that is.

Miz Dora Scott was fun to watch unlike Dennis she dressed
allll the way up nice hat down to her tiny tipalong feet never
rushed always calling out at 103 to Elvira then moving on
that pocketbook on her right arm justa shakin with palsy
Miz Dora spoke & visited & walked til she cldnt no more
if we needed to go somewhere we walked. That's how we
used to do it. Wanna go somewhere, walk,
like i might circle the lake then walk on up to Atlanta & see
my nephew Jud turn around & be back by dark.

●

unnameable

splenderiferously grand wahtasplexdoriferous

waadoblextropobal!
ywetherollink!   Ahhhhhh thrgnenen.
Ah thracklespurtz.

●

Fathers' Day (for D. Patton & Lisa Saurez)

Testosterone thugs
sperm bank donors. danger:
Goddess forgotten.

●

Another Sunday @ the lake

out early enuf the
sour-faced natives all in church.
ducks & geese wth eating disorders
rising humidity & temperatures

Allelujah.   Alleluyah.

●

"And still, we rise"

i sorrow for those of us stricken prematurely
by thickened abdomens, thighs,
stomachs & waists wider than our
ample delicious dessert behinds

i feel sorrow & pride for our thickening selves
encased in inarticulate grief, one-way righteous rage
turned main course endless meal of carbohydrates &
comfort foods yet out here today
in a warm lake breeze creating our own
slipstreams of joy. *Ahshay.*

●

sacred space small depot

room two wimmin with
the same name same purpose

seniors elders raise
hands to proudly tell age, dates
of time seamless faces engraved

sunsets as we walk
Level Grove cemetery
sacred sweat wine love

●

Invocation (29/3/2011)

(for Asungi & Sunni P.)

earth
air

water
fire

air
earth
water
fire

poems travel lengths of longest locks

earth come air lift
raise be transport for head, feet honey relief in
dreams actualized come Zora,
come Miz Ida B Wells
come on Dr. Margaret Walker again
& again be this buoyant air this sacred earth sandy
brown blessed loam softened by drizzle lake water enhanced
soft chill ripples borne eastward from a hidden sun
come air
come earth
come Nina, please. ("Call the Spirits & make 'um run.") come all.
air
earth water
i am the fire. i am fire.

●

for Zelda Lee (& her knee operations)

(May 12, 2011)

and as you submerge go under
soft waterfalls ocean waves purge
putrescent exhaustion
alien aggravations primordial pain
dictatorial delusional endless to-do lists
laugh going under &

emerge painfree, joyously triumphant
re-kneed, renewed re-you'd

●

can't get away from

that image
of eyes glued
wide open on a
searing hot sky

burned in truth
still seeing truth

•

Thursday: for Oya, Damballah, Chango

green beige purple & white
by these colors led to
what's right for the rest of my life

white & purple, beige green
purple green. beige white
reaching in delight

a spell to call what needs to be
Damballah Oya Chango hear
me yr daughter incarnate : red

recall install invest
after i forget who where what
i AM Obeah. i be obeah oh Mami i
have done time

green. today's red. beige. purple. white.
yes yes & also (always) write.

•

when I see the word
lover I think of you

•

85 degrees already out here at 10:30a.m.
just walk fast don't think about heat
hurricanes promised tornado twisted Tuscaloosa
contest St Loo & Joplin Missouri wimmin raped &
tortured repeatedly in the Congo in my neighborhood
85 degrees wth a breeze if i cld i wld donate more dodge
all the bullets of whtmale supremacy & other
manifestations of hate mail of bouncing mutations
of fat cells jiggling in my overheated brain

•

today is (for Gil Scott-Heron 28 May 2011)

yellowwhite grief
streaked with golden purple
Gil-grief where *did* our times go
going on going on this great
communal grief the soundz of millions mourning

•

the farmvle blues

oh. i got th fv blues & can't be
satisfied. (repeat)
woke up ths morning feeling fine
til i got to that ole farm o mine
where they got me hogtied
wanting more than i can spend:
50 dollars usd to expand and then -
go to the 2nd farm & more of th same & email
wants me to save the wolves.
feed the hongry in Haiti
save th wimmn in th dnc
ignore this whtmale s.o.b.

standing in my path dlibrately
tryn to oh irridescent green duck feathers 2nd loop keep
going & going tryn to guilt me abt the world's needs
now the dn party & campaign 2012. give give give the
changeverything.org. the LBGT the
UNCC. & NAACP & NOTNOWNOHOW
oh why can't i jst expand my farms, learn this keyboard,
avoid these tree trunks but. nooo
its Sunday morning time to repent pretend to relent
in sin, foolishness & sloth.forgive me tree. i did not see u
and oh these farmvle expansion blues
these strong
strong, tenacious roots.

●

ascent

Erik Satie piano music poem

la la, la la la
la la la la la
(laaaaaaaa laaaaaaaaaaaa
laaaaaaaaa la)

glimmering desire
effervescent sparkle.
That glow. That fire.

hurry hurry stop.
rush rush don't be
late for what
ever that was.

dawn.
twilight.
dusk.

dawn. sunrise.
sunset. twilight
dusk.

Toni Morrison's observation that there is *no* memorial

(plaque/ statue / bench/marker) - nothing to commemorate our Enslaved Ancestors, complete erasure ("found" in Angelyn Mitchell's *The Freedom to Remember* p. 144)

but Toni -
as 'Zake wrote in *Sassafras, Cypress & Indigo,*
"the slaves who are ourselves" - we are the
living memorials. living memorials & re-memories.

Shhhh.   Silence.
Come everyone sit here in this carved
moment with its plaque "In Grateful Memory of
the Enslaved Africans who built my house, my life, my family,
my fortune, this town / city / country."

This is a major historical commemoration.

My sister Dolores' Birthday

> *"Be careful what you wish for . . .   /   History starts now."*
> *song on radio*

Pastel golden orange early
morning you are
up already

staring in a silver mirror
to mull over your
teeth (white), eyes (brown), life

smiling or oblivious
make a wry face &
back to blue
bedroom & dress green
for work this
is your history, this

is you, purple, as i
walk this treadmill

thirty lavender minutes
my mind and heart

smile its your
birthday and again
your history starts -
now, red.
go.

Song under the Stillman Magnolias (Commencement 2008)

And i have sought
you in the morning, to
have you all day

when the morning
was beginning to
find, therein, a way

again, i will seek
you every morning
and all day until

i am your
Sunrise to
illuminate each day.

that epic southern novel i promised you, compressed

Sitting here in this doctor's office waiting for this life changing or at least altering event, ponder the possibilities the range of realities - can i play the piano afterwards? (Doc says yes emphatically) the saxophone? Will someone still want to hug & kiss me a little maybe on the cheek? Most importantly most importantly what happened to that small deer standing skittish over in the woods two days ago?

And what was that road kill laid out this morning, a tail with rings around it - raccoon or possum? Well it seems i have at last chosen the right dentist that is, according to my white, down-to-earth late 30's orthodontist's assistant who thinks the other dentist (regular, to pull an extra tooth) and i will "geehaw" then quickly corrected "oh that is not a good thing to say" but it's okay i said as we all three talk at once she starts to explain the word but i know

Because Daddy John, my granddaddy Daddy John was always gee hawing something, or someone behind some kinda ole sorry mule, out there behind 103 Soque Street in a bright soft summer sun, stubbornly pushing a plow through chunky red dirt, sweat rolling down his dark brown face, streaking his worn coveralls dark blue, gee haw! gee haw! gee haw! with a look on his face that said "dammit" while he trained that plow. Gee haw. Gee haw. i wanna tell this little round orthodontist i got to get this done & git on to work.

And see to this whole set-up, situation changed, altered, with the entrance of Soque Street and *that* is what Appalachia will do you; what happens when the mountains inside start telling stories some you know you know, like Sheila K. Adams, and some, you know, the mountains know.

Gee Haw, Daddy John. Dammit, git a move on, Dr. Orthodontist, time's a wasting. Which digressed us slightly from a succinct statement of yesterday's visits (oh check out that soft sibilant sound rolling thru here - *surely* that counts, Tiara, for something. Let's have some more: *surely*.)

What, then, is objectively correlative to a giant, body-sized smile? Oh now, pretty, skinny dark-skinned sister / French manicured *toe* nails pretty as they can be but kinda long

Chapter 15: This morning i watched T. Hoagland put a cement truck in his poem witnessed the weight, size, the well - concreteness. Inspired by such inventiveness i think Hmmm. Try this: Metal-Mouth Womon. No. Metallic Womon. Better. Magnetized Old Womon (MOW)
Lu wld say, she of the regular mouth with normal teeth - which she swears i have more than (teeth) and big too.
Get in here: full weight of this metal brace protruding my lips, lacerating the skin behind, like this high pressure system of clouded-in-150% humidity hovers in smotheration over Albany, how this metal, this morning, presses & smothers my soul. Discomfort so unique, definite, defying any adequate description these braces, this second morning. Who knew a

Croissant could be so *muscular* ? Fighting back - springing up, like a cheap cut of beef shank, the kind we useta have, years ago, on Sunday, with carrots, potatoes, onions & cook all day to tenderize & it's still tough, this croissant challenges my ability to chew metallically. good thing i got this coffee.

(Hoagland = p.118, April Poetry Calendar, 2007, Alhambra Publishing)

to Audrey in Savannah

Come. Down to the
waterfront & find
a space for us a
table outside
cappuccino, *biscotti*
smiles &
discuss how we want
the world to be
this sparkly day.
Come on. Let's go down
to a waterfront cafe
just you & me
today.

Bo Didley dead today at age 79

"Distant Lover" live
on the radio coming
down Pine into Turtle Park
dark green tops
of freshly washed
trees rhythm,
rightness and you,
Earl King, somewhere
in an eternal hot summer, having
an endless barbecue with extra cold beer
in perpetual summer greenness
in our George Washington Carver Park
singing Bo Didley. Ohhhh Bo Didley.

people watch # 7

only one trimmed
down sleek
economy size in here.

all the rest of us super-sized
wide-loads, RV plus 4's
too-many-fries-with-that-shake
comfortably cushioned
family sized 10 tons of
fun

●

a september song:

i went on
vacation in May
forgot to
tell me to come
back.

i let my mind go on
vacation in May
forgot to tell it when
to come back.
forgot to tell me,
come back.

●

a Pilates Method approach

Instead of sometimes,
us both being bent
by assorted (sordid)
weights bowed, separately
stoop shouldered let's,
sometimes, exchange the
heaviness, straighten,
stretch out to each other,
contract - from that core -
smile, release.

●

Do not intend to get "old" - won't die until this
new brown tea pot makes 2 thousand
pots of green tea & another million of teeccinno
coffee substitute. Won't even want to die until

i dance a dance for every chance i
had to hug someone i loved.
i won't die or even feel like it until i
sang 20 loud annoying songs to Lu on the

telephone, choreograph ten performances for my
Slinky and me, lasso the full moon and ride from

here to Sylva. (And you - you *are* my "bucket
list.") So - don't even think about going there.
Don't even try.

6 June 2008

Peeps calling each other up -
you got yr license yet?
I got mine! See ya later!
Celebrating California's new law:
we Lesbians & Gays, LGBT's,
can be openly licensed,
legally married to each other
i sent a happydance e-mail
to Viv, to Lee, what else, here,
can i do? Call Sharon.
Reckon Karen got his license?
Move back home to Los Angeles.
(if i had stayed, if my Cheryl &
it would be more than
30 years now we could get
married, like hets).

Maybe i could move back today,
line up in that queue,
wait for some likely womon &
ask her to marry me for a day
reckon Keith got her license?

If i had stayed.
would be more than 30 years
but now we can get married,
just   like   hets ?

A Summer Solstice

Distances deceive
in any direction wide open flat
green fields, sunrise sudden pecan
groves in front lawns where
others stick a hot-pink flamingo
but delete *that* image and go on,
let's go on into

These deceptive
distances of time
and time again for my wimmin,
past & everpresent

Chocolate, Mab S, Sherry, Adella
Adella, Kay B, AfraShe, Viv,
JeanKnee, bella, Connie C & Connie L you
know who you are: a feast

Highly-seasoned black eyed peas
& potatoes prepared back in
April, frozen for now Goddess,
bless this feast of friendship &
like my peas & do,
stay spicy, hot
& filling, forever.

●

for Li Ch'ing - Chao *(ca. 1084 - 1151I; NAL Vol. B p.1408)*

Two big drops of wet, muggy
salty sweat descend
(drop / plop) on page 1420
of my *Norton Anthology of World Literature*.
Blasphemy. (Water on a book.)

Having just read, reverently,
your words of futile
passion for material possessions,
particularly words carved on stone,
i smirk, self-mocking,
almost twist an ankle,
on this fast treadmill and
tenderly dry this precious book.

●

task:

Find the Lei Lines.
Play them.
Be them.

●

Beach Blues (motel rooms $109-125 per on a Wednesday night in July)

Oh shut up look up beaches on the internet put
yrelf in the picture. put on yr new black slinky

fat-ladies' skirt swim suit & get in the shower
& do the breast stroke (drink salt water 1st) &
swim, swim, swim!

You can cover 10-20 beaches for the price of
none; international, local, *private*, whatever - in
the time it takes to gas up (& for a fraction of
the cost) you can have more than twenty
beaches discovered, visited, *cached*. Put a
sock in it. Hush.

•

New bumper sticker (Aug. 2008)

My niece Ani is a Las Vegas Showgirl & she just graduated
from the Univ. of the Arts in Pennsylvania (BFA Modern
Dance). what chu got?

•

Honorific parody of Maya Angelou's "Still I Rise"

Fibromyalgia grabbed &
slapped me back down on
the bed. At first i thought -
lower back! Lawd no -
it was my head around C2.
And still, i walk.

Plantar fasciitis in the left foot,
wobblies in both knees,

MC salt flush while reading a
Japanese short story too many
to do's & still, i walk.

Almost at door bio-freeze foot
no jacket chilly two cloth bags
in trunk go back & no no now
sun burns high traffic blinds ears

Crossing five streams of traffic,
anxiety of whiteracist motorists
running me down in my Obama
shirt / quickly sprint across to the
church & walk west on Gillionville one vertebrae
at a time through mid-back
rib dislocation (sharp pain with
each breath) i walk. i walk
past a boil a huge pimple
on my . . . *privates*

Fasciitis pain (again & again),
both feet drizzling rain &
a one inch round dark brown spider
soon dead and still, i walked.

●

Incident at a Red light

(Slappey & Pine, Albany, GA)

Stopped about 5:30 pm at the intersection red light & in the
left turning lane, a vintage beatup dark blue with dented rust
spots, small pickup truck and two brothers - the one on the
passenger side old(er) tired looking, deep, deep brown,
experienced-etched face we looked at

each other - so close, cld have reached over and shook
hands so we locked eyes & nodded in a friendly distant
polite & ain't it a hot, tired, glad-to-be-going-home Friday
evening kinda way & i slid into a pleasant stroll way
back down my mind's memory to Maxine's daddy's
pick-up truck in Augusta and how i missed him, missed
them, the driver leaned over the other and spoke: "How you
doing ma'am." i smiled. "Is yo' husband married?" he leers,
the other one grins.
"No, i shot him," i say. and smile. They don't.
Both heads whip straight ahead, truck burns rubber
left as the red light shifts bright green.

"Come back. Come back" i call. laughing.
"i shot him. He dead. i need another one.
 How 'bout you?"

●

2 November 2008

Sun rises
in blue, white, red
(in this poem)

The Obama logo sun
rises steadily over this
duplex, this land, the world,
it is a good day.
a good morning.
in *this* poem.

●

Conversation with a ladybug ("Good luck if you see one, if one lights on you.")

an orange-red tinyspot of comatosity,
on my airless desk in this
sunbaked, stale aired classroom,
she seemed unconscious, dead

until i prodded her, politely, with a
left index finger. then tiny black
feeler feet emerged, moved,
weakly she pulled herself up my finger

like it was a rubber raft lifesaver in a rough ocean
floating wood in the debris
of her own mini Titanic, like
my finger was a lost & feared

gone forever friend she'd waited so long for,
she clung tenaciously to my
finger, roamed slowly its
surface as i lifted her tenderly

outside to air but
she held tight had to
prise her off & onto the
shrub-tree deep orange autumn
leaf outside Holley Hall suddenly
she flew. away.

●

TRUST

but this, i think, i know about you, if you condescended to play
that get-to-know-yr colleagues group game, that dangerous
touchy-feely one where a person freefalls back into the arms
of someone she trusts will catch her - like i told Sherley &
Frances a few days ago when that

subject somehow came up (no telling what will when Frances
shows up) i said to them i said, i admire those that play *that*
game but me - no. Heretofore. i know i can be relied on
to catch whoever i can, back and head *very* strong, reliable,
resilient hands, i am

a good catcher but as for me / give me a strong wind, a clear
space, an *idea* to fall back on & there you go so - don't go.
wait - where was i ? Here. With you. That was then.

Subsequent events have transpired to transform my perception.
You. You, i believe, if you stand behind me, in that game, if i
know it is you, *then* i might cld relax completely & fall into
your hands & arms, i wld commend myself to the *idea* that you
would catch me or that you might catch me i do trust you really,
really i do to catch me unless

that is, you have a board meeting, a cabinet meeting, a one-on-
one, a fire to put out or bank, a loved one to castigate / direct /
appease/ propitiate; an event or speech to over-prepare for, an
incoming "got to take this" cell phone call, a traveling event,
on the road, unless it is not a good time, not in conflict with
anything on that ultimate calendar, then. Yes. You. Only.

●

assent

Slowly turned right off 441-N on to
Dillsboro's Main Street deep into the sun setting
mountain greying mountain time evening
slowly, wearily, gratefully turned right

Thru holiday decorations still up
bright red banners on lightposts
just at that second, "Diagon Alley"
from John Williams' Harry Potter 1
soundtrack started.

But. you need to know that music totally,
intimately, precisely, you would need to know
each nuanced inflection of variations on Hedwig's
theme from the introduction to the change of season
and Dumbledore's first appearance with the putter-outer you,

You oh-so-condescending adult - & therefore two times
muggle, do not dare say you listened to
some of it / yr grandkids / an acquaintance who
plays 3rd violin in Williams' orchestra, or
-worst - "I just never got in to HP" (then i can't get into you)
so - that - hopefully said, and done : whazza
matta witchu? Go. Get. the. soundtrack. now.

You would need to know - you would
have to know, even more than my tranced
drive up Soque Street for the first time in 3 1/2
years a few miles earlier (plus need to know what *that* means)
to understand - Diagon Alley's music
as i only a few feet from

Enchanted Sylva with small decorated
& lit trees around hilltop city hall
& on a bench near the old library,
two young whitmales sit playing a banjo
& a fiddle. (And Howard's Grocery Store
still open.) You need to know how Hagrid
& Harry performed magic on ordinary red
bricks / opened an alternate reality as
my magic cabbage sister opened this one
you need to know my mountains hear them
speak know the soundtrack, movie,
book & first of all, my Soque
Street from then to now oh you so
need (to know) all of that
to even ever hear this.

self-affirmation ?

battering metal &
wire inside my
mouth expensive alien
invasion: braces
at age 59
then foot surgery on
right foot - metal
screw insert in big
toe / bone shaved
behind smallest metatarsal
limited mobility for
months / no exercise for
6, as muscles atrophy
my smile goes into
retirement behind
rubber bands and i

love myself ??

poem @ 60 / 60 yr old poem

consider its eyes'
gleam: knowingly enticingly

bicepped hug muscles
ready for the next

quarter century
thighs clenched
to sprint / or
hold

...the mere thought of

you one day *thinking* about
putting an arm
around my waist motivates
me to get one (a waist)

and i got a ph.d for this

Reluctantly awake to must-do's got to's care for teeth gum disease brush floss gargle with nasty-mint tasting mouthwash hope the 6 cm hole in gum is helped by now it's 6:30 a.m. instead of 5 & sit & slowly computer on / ice the right surgeried foot, wrap ice pack around still swollen pad of big toe, stretches to right outside over the not-yet-healed-hump then hurt myself with sadistic exercises bending that toe to the front back, back until i sweat & cry out Oh! Oh! Oh & maybe try to keep this master cleanse all these toxins must go drink 32 oz of sea salt water check the clock check the oh no - & still one set of papers to grade for Freshman comp II at 3 p.m. or maybe do them @ 10, 1, & 3 if i stay until 6 all these papers oh no look at the clock okay okay iced foot, exercises, emails checked now shower, quickly dry off rush

get dressed this chafing, too tight bra - no wire but totally oppressive cutting into my flesh b/c these new full breasts might excite someone's lust or censure okay okay then more flesh binding queen size panty hose roll up the legs one side wrong leg look at clock re-do careful with the foot, the time the time whew now a full slip in case the dress is see-thru & camouflage what is natural in a more rational world cater to this backwards double double (non)standard for BlackWimmin academics at Black colleges in the deepsouth oh please let's admit what everyone knows: antebellum neo- fascist enslavement to outdated mores

more honest, convenient & comfortable to dress *purdah* but now, sausaged up dressed down thick hot socks to protect right foot thick gym shoes for support by doctor's orders only 3 more torturous months (& 1 more year with the metal teeth oops: forgot rubber bands) and hurrah almost hmmm 5 bracelets to left arm 2 can cover that sist on inside right wrist at the spot where i severed a tendon doesn't seem to be growing mash it down but it

pops back up hurts some bracelets there & 2 rings a crystal, a jade; right hand amber, grab the book bag, Tilly hat & sun glasses for eye sensitivity open door - chilly - get denim rain coat & shawl & again, door. and

20 min erratic traffic going 20-55 mph in 45 mph zone. and there. Here in a temporary office in the freshman women's dormitory to meet a youngmale football player (who plagiarized once already) and tediously, laboriously, teach him, from 9-9:45 a.m. how to construct a thesis sentence for a two page composition. Well. At last. He got it.

Rubber rain boots with roses

A group photo with me to the
right of Charles - & Helen, & Mildred
amazing - i stand there
all in one piece and still
(but all the pieces of me wobble when i move)

The fat pores of my body
seep sideways through my
skin, amorphously heavy losing
shape like some retarded succubus
or night traveling shape-shifter
too trifling to do it right.

Feels like i ooze, formless,
through days & nights
led by a pulsating lack
of physical shape or purpose. amazing.

and that is quite enough / of *that*.

> *"I got things to do . . . work in the garden if it ever stops raining."*
> - *my Cabbage Sis one day in late May*

Ain't it raining, though?

Seems like the ground
would be gone everywhere
seem like we would
all be swimming or else
growing gills. Yes, gills -
like fish, so we could
swim you could swim
around your cabbages
tend to your Atlantis herbs
& pour out sunshine
from a can (sold by volume, not weight)
soon won't hafta weed no
more - they'd all just
float up out the ground,
wiggle on off. Like worms & water snakes.
What? Oh. But

yeah - it sure is raining -
it really *is* coming down.

my new tattoo at 4 weeks & 1 day old

overpriced, overcharged
(it's Asheville, whadya expect?)
its colors blend into mine
& from a slight distance -
my head to my right
shoulder, where the tattoo is -
it's all a greyish band bleeding
hot pink, mostly hidden
by t-shirt sleeves but yeah:

now *these* mountains
are truly mine. Permanent &
forever.

●

a smile before
9 a.m. is as
efficacious as a vitamin pill

a grin, going into 10 (a.m.), just as
gregarious as
a 5 mile run
endorphins line up,
just the same,
cholesterol dips
and so on
& on

●

Aw hell, EB (*for Ethelbert & all his talk abt the "5th Inning"*)

Maybe, EB, you got a point.
i measure my mortality by all of ours.
the quick hurtful surprise
shock denial another
us gone: Nina, Miriam, Lucille –
Jo Carson yes our stars and
kin, like cousins
i tear up & got chills on
"trying to keep spirits
up" trying, myself see
that gentle night try to
embrace me, settle down softly
on our generation
and - y'know - i
had foot surgery?
But much as i danced, kicked ass -
yes. well. i know what you mean
even if baseball never made much
sense to me (sorry) still, i
sense an *inning* at each day's
end each sunset each
oh hell yes and yet i say,

play on. Let's adamantly play. On

maps

*nice to see where you
might end up at if
you keep going past
where you headed*

for us

(AfraShe Asungi, Vivian P & Jean P)

Like a strong thick blue rubber band
holding fresh organic broccoli or
a well travelled road
with new smooth blacktop

●

Sixty grey and brown
geese sailed slowly
east on the lake merged
into glittery sunlight

●

ascent

Put on my favorite hi-top shoes
big oversized stretched out
faded purple sweatshirt
baggy grey sweat pants, shades
sun hat. Go

out the back door.
Leave it unlocked.
Leave it unlocked but closed
and walk away.

Start walking.
Keep on walking.

Dedication

Dedicated to everyone whose name i called or mentioned and especially to Audrey Davenport, my (new) nephew Fredric Bembry, Jimmie & Richard Tinius, and my ROOTs daughters: Ebonie K. Miles, Jade Laren, Kelly Thomas, Marquetta Dupree, and Rebecca Mwase.

Above L/R: Ebonie, Marquetta, doris, Rebecca (Photo: Margo Miller)

Kelly Thomas (Photo: Autumn Williams, age 10)

Jade Laren (Facebook Photo; permission requested)

about the author

doris davenport is a writer, educator, and literary & performance poet with degrees from Paine College (B.A. English), SUNY Buffalo (M.A. English) and the University of Southern California (Ph.D. Literature). doris has done more than 150 poetry performances and workshops including a collaborative performance ("Conversations With Time") at ROOTsFest in June 2011 in Baltimore, MD. She has published book reviews, articles, essays, and eight books of poetry. From Aug. 2007 - May 2011, doris was an Associate Professor of English at Albany State University (Albany, GA), where she coordinated the Annual Poetry Festival, for four consecutive years. Presently, she is happily back home at Stillman in Tuscaloosa, AL as Associate Professor of English. doris helped organize an open mic at Stillman for the international event on Sept. 24, 2011 "100,000 Poets for Change." And on Oct. 15, 2011, she participated, as an invited author, in the 13th Annual Georgia Literary Festival in Sautee-Nacoochee, GA.

Memberships: College Language Association (CLA), ALTERNATE Roots, MELUS, National Writers' Union (NWU). More information: http://www.redroom.com/author/doris-diosa-davenport

Contact information: zorahpoet7@gmail.com